STORYLAND

2

Student's Book

Lisiane Ott Schulz

Luciana Santos Pinheiro

Storyland Student's Site Access Code:
Storyland2@students

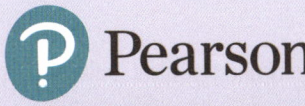

Head of Product - Pearson Brasil	Juliano Costa
Product Manager - Pearson Brasil	Marjorie Robles
Product Coordinator - ELT	Mônica Bicalho
Authors	Lisiane Ott Schulz
	Luciana Santos Pinheiro
Collaborators	Fernanda Bressan Capelini
	Indiana Oliveira
	Milena Schneid Eich
	Sofia Xanthopoulos Bordin
	Verônica Bombassaro
Editor - ELT	Simara H. Dal'Alba
Editorial Assistant - ELT	Sandra Vergani Dall'Agnol
Proofreader	Silva Serviços de Educação
Proofreader (Portuguese):	Fernanda R. Braga Simon
Copyeditor	Maria Estela Alcântara
Teacher's Guide (Portuguese translation)	Eduardo Lubisco Portella
Pedagogical Reviewer	Márcia Marques Goulart
Quality Control	Renata S. C. Victor
Product Design Coordinator	Rafael Lino
Art Editor - ELT	Emily Andrade
Production Editors	Daniel Reis
	Vitor Martins
Acquisitions and permissions Manager	Maiti Salla
Acquisitions and permissions	Sandra Sebastião
Graphic design	Mirella Della Maggiore Armentano
	APIS design integrado
Graphic design (cover)	Daniel Reis
	Emily Andrade
	Mirella Della Maggiore Armentano
Illustration (cover)	Leandro Marcondes
Illustrated by	Alex Cói	Estúdio Secreto
	Bruna Sousa
	Dayane Cabral
	Leandro Marcondes
	Mari Heffner
	Victor Lemos
Content Development	Allya Language Solutions
Media Development	Estação Gráfica
Audio	Maximal Studio

Every effort has been made to trace the copyright holders and we apologize in advance for any unintentional omissions. We would be pleased to insert the appropriate acknowledgement in any subsequent edition of this publication.

Dados Internacionais de Catalogação na Publicação (CIP)
(Câmara Brasileira do Livro, SP, Brasil)

Schulz, Lisiane Ott
    Storyland 2: Student's Book / Lisiane Ott Schulz, Luciana Santos Pinheiro ; [coordenação Monica Bicalho]. -- 1. ed. -- São Paulo : Pearson Education do Brasil, 2018.

Vários ilustradores.
ISBN 978-85-430-2630-5

1. Inglês (Educação infantil) I. Pinheiro, Luciana Santos. II. Bicalho, Monica. III. Título.

18-17170   CDD-372.21

Índices para catálogo sistemático:
1. Inglês : Educação infantil 372.21
Maria Alice Ferreira - Bibliotecária - CRB-8/7964

ISBN 978-85-430-2630-5 (Student's Book)

STORYLAND

Student's Book 2

UNIT 1	GOLDILOCKS AND THE THREE BEARS	8
UNIT 2	THE TORTOISE AND THE HARE	16
UNIT 3	JACK AND JILL	24
UNIT 4	THE THREE LITTLE PIGS	32
UNIT 5	THE LITTLE RED HEN	40
UNIT 6	HANSEL AND GRETEL	48
UNIT 7	PINOCCHIO	56
UNIT 8	THE ANT AND THE GRASSHOPPER	64

PRESS-OUTS 73

STICKERS 89

Scope and Sequence

UNIT	THEME	VALUES	OBJECTIVES	MAIN LANGUAGE	SONG	CLIL
1 Goldilocks And The Three Bears	Family	Respect other people's belongings	• Distinguish between *big* and *small* • Identify and name family members • Describe the elements in a house	baby, brother, dad, girl, grandma, grandpa, mom, sister; chair, house; big, good, hard, hot, little, soft, small; This chair is small.	There was a little girl	Art: Make a bed for Goldilocks
2 The Tortoise And The Hare	At the Playground	Play together. Respect differences	• Name playground equipment • Distinguish between *fast* and *slow* • Name primary colors	play; fast, slow; see-saw, slide, swing; blue, red, yellow; playground; rain, sun; What's this? What color is this? Who is fast?	Rain, rain, go away	Art & Math: Make color cup prints
3 Jack And Jill	Community	Cooperate and work together; Ask adults for help	• Identify and name community helpers • Count to five	baker, firefighter, nurse, police officer; one, two, three, four, five; Can you count to five?	Do you know the muffin man?	Cooking: Make chocolate truffles
4 The Three Little Pigs	Home Shapes and colors	There is a time to play and there is a time to work	• Name shapes and house materials • Identify and name primary and secondary colors • Count to six	house, brick, straw, wood; circle, oval, rectangle, square, triangle; blue, green, red, orange, yellow; It's a red triangle.	In a cabin in the woods	Art: Build houses

UNIT	THEME	VALUES	OBJECTIVES	MAIN LANGUAGE	SONG	CLIL
5 The Little Red Hen	Animals	Respect differences and be friends	• Identify and name farm animals	cat, chick, cow, duck, dog, hen, pig; farm, farmer	Old MacDonald	Art & Craft: Make a pig
6 Hansel And Gretel	Food	Avoid risky situations	• Distinguish between healthy and unhealthy food	apple, banana, bread, cake, candy, cookies, fruit, milk; blue, green, orange, purple, red, yellow; teacup, teapot rainbow	I'm a little teapot	Art & Science: Make a paper rainbow
7 Pinocchio	My Body	Tell the truth	• Identify and name parts of the body • Distinguish between *short* and *long*, and *right* and *left*	arms, body, eyes, ears, foot, feet, hands, head, legs, nose; left, right; long, short; How many? Is it long or short?	Hokey Pokey	Art & Science: Make a Pinocchio puppet
8 The Ant And The Grasshopper	Seasons	Be responsible	• Identify and name the four seasons • Identify and name animals • Name colors	fall, spring, cold, hot; summer winter; ant, crocodile, elephant, grasshopper, bear, skunk; What animal is this? Which season is it?	If you should meet an elephant	Art & Math: Make hand print trees

3 CUT AND GLUE.

LESSON 2

4 LOOK AND TRACE.

5 LOOK, LISTEN, AND SING.

LESSON 3

 **6** LOOK, DRAW, AND COLOR.

 LESSON 3

7 LISTEN AND CIRCLE.

LESSON 4

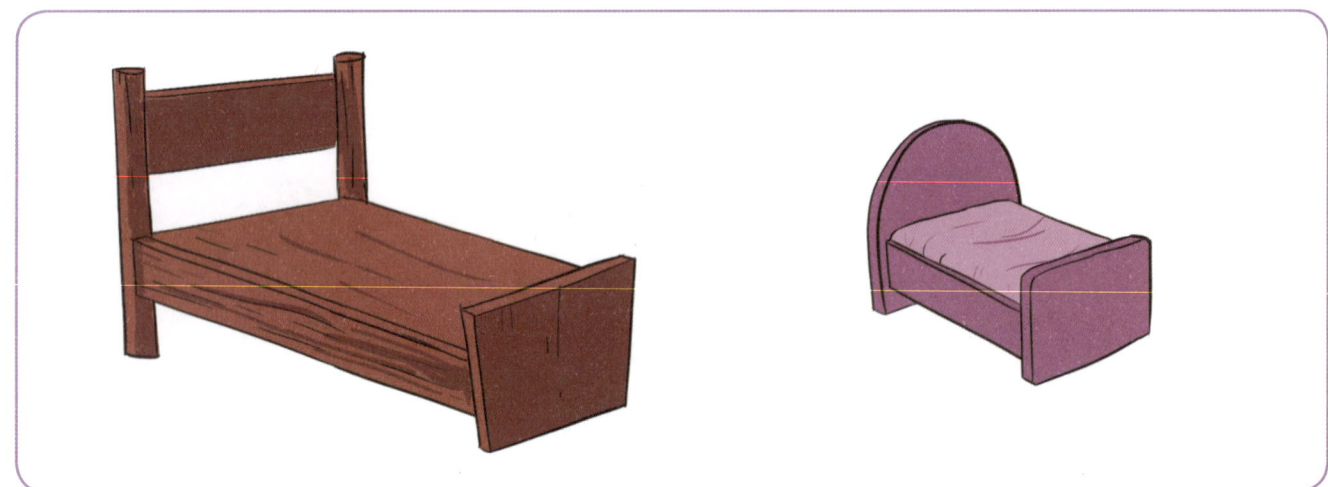

8 MAKE A BED FOR GOLDILOCKS.

ART & SOCIAL STUDIES · CLIL · LESSON 4

6 LISTEN AND SING. TRACK 08

7 GLUE AND SAY.

2 LISTEN AND ACT OUT. TRACK 09

LESSON 1

3 LOOK AND MATCH.

Lesson 2

 CUT, GLUE, AND SAY.

5 LOOK, SAY, AND DRAW.

LESSON 3

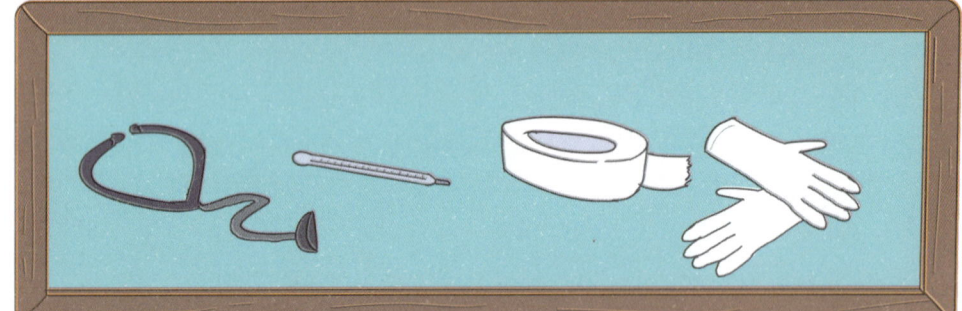

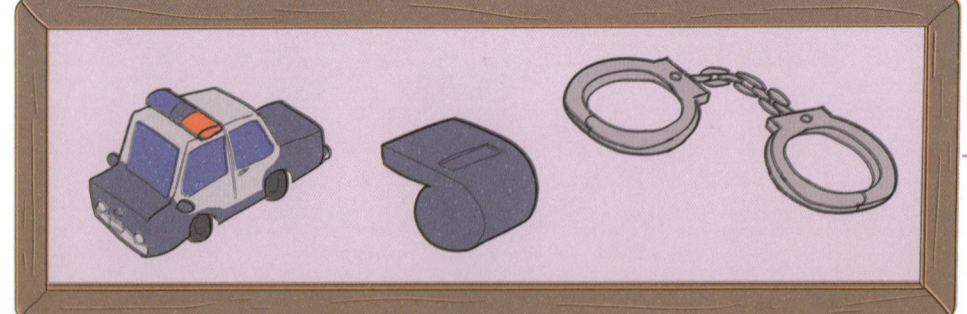

6 LISTEN AND SING. TRACK 10

LESSON 3

 **7** LISTEN AND CIRCLE.

8 MAKE CHOCOLATE TRUFFLES.

COOKING CLIL · LESSON 4

2 LISTEN, STICK, AND ACT OUT.

3. LISTEN, POINT, AND COLOR.  TRACK 13

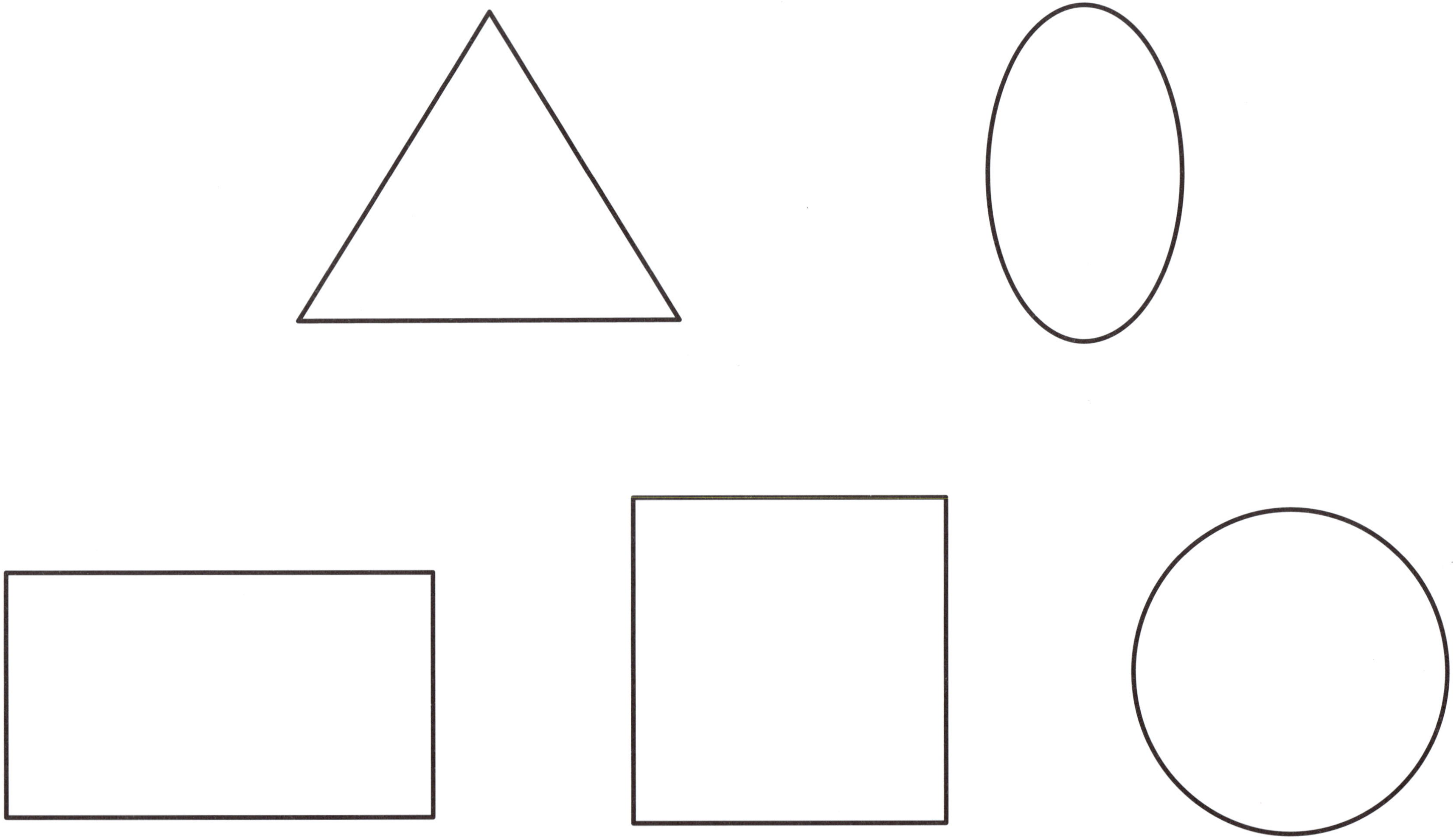

LESSON 2

4 LOOK AND DRAW.

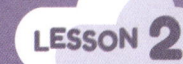

5 LISTEN, SING, AND ACT OUT.

6 LISTEN, ORDER, AND GLUE.

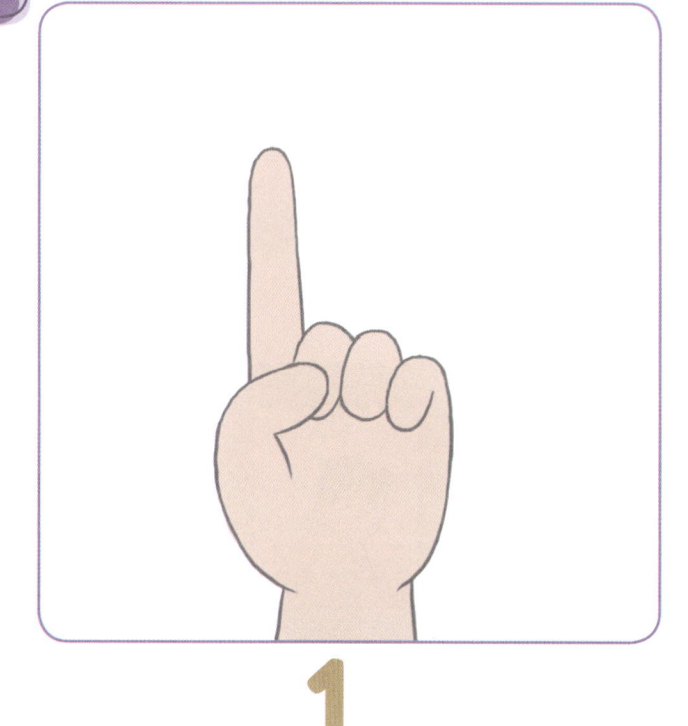

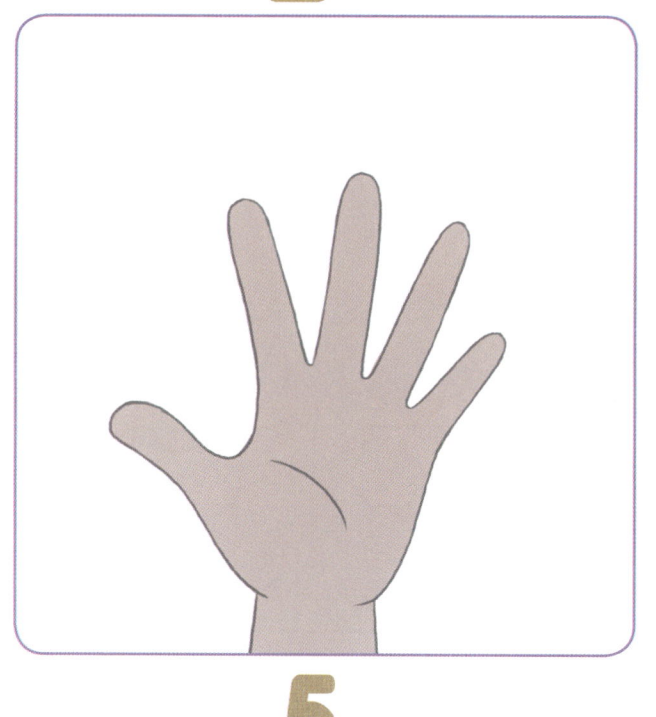

TRACK 15

Lesson 3

1

2

3

4

5

6

7 POINT, SAY, AND TRACE.

8 BUILD HOUSES.

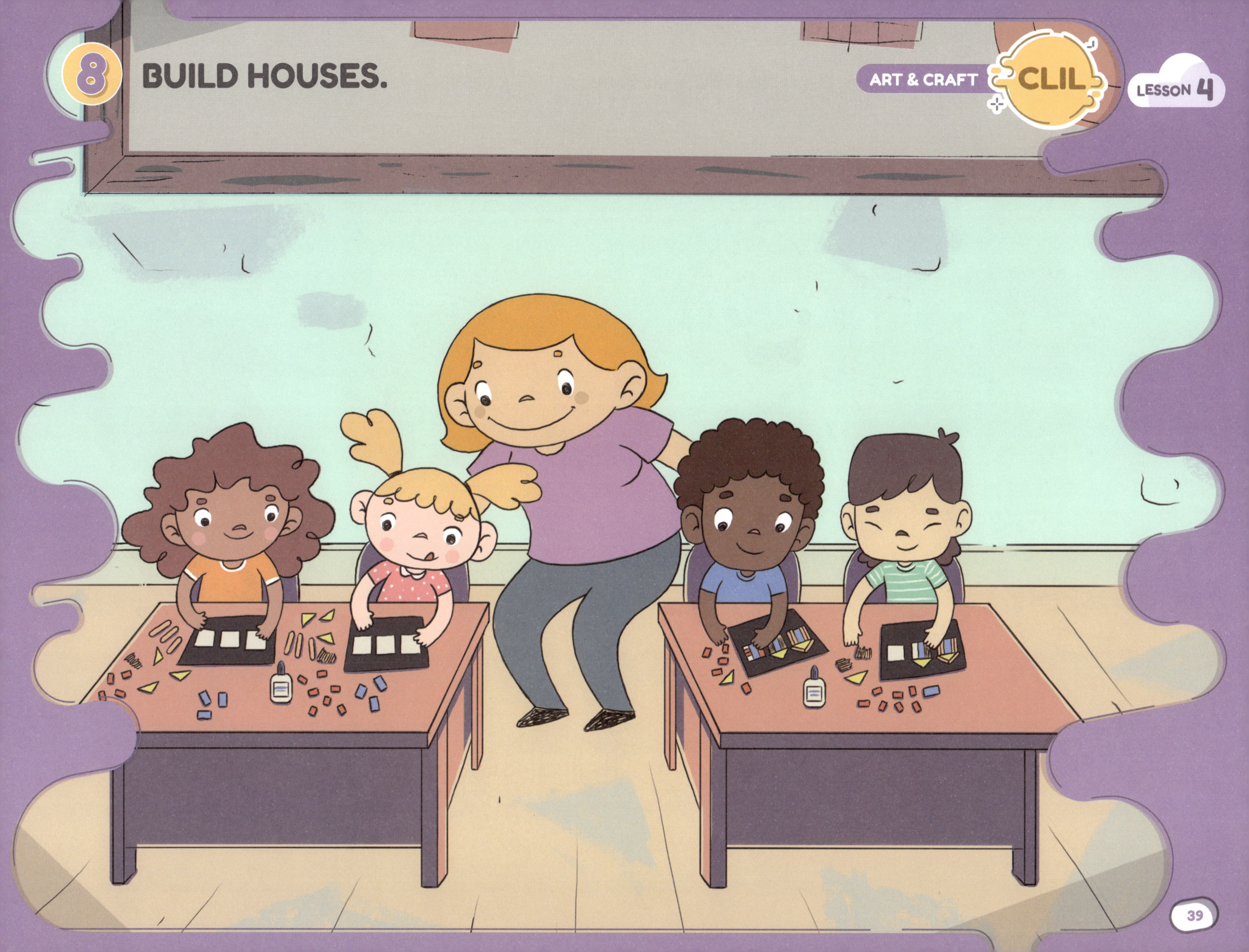

ART & CRAFT CLIL LESSON 4

UNIT 5 — The Little Red Hen

LESSON 1

1. LOOK AND CIRCLE.

2 LISTEN AND STICK.

TRACK 16

LESSON 1

STORY

3 LOOK, MATCH, AND SAY.

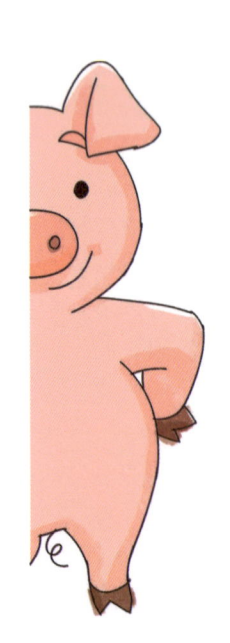

LESSON 2

4 CUT, ORDER, AND GLUE.

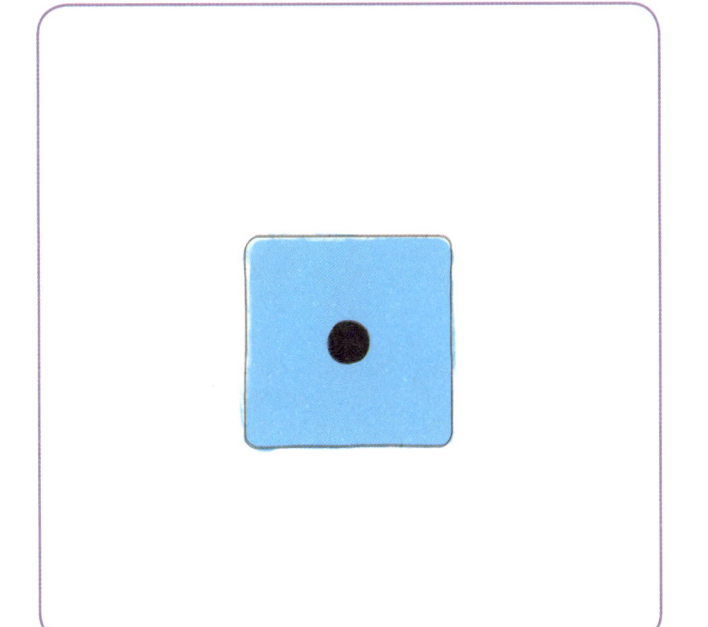

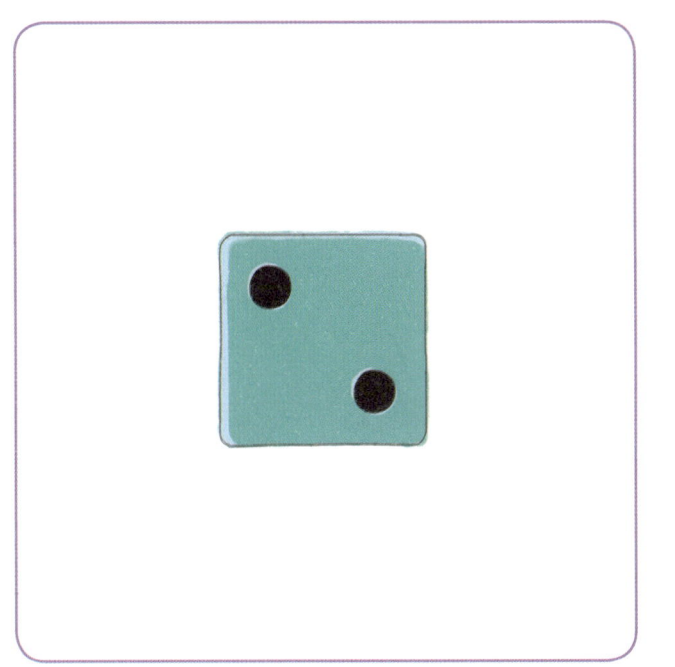

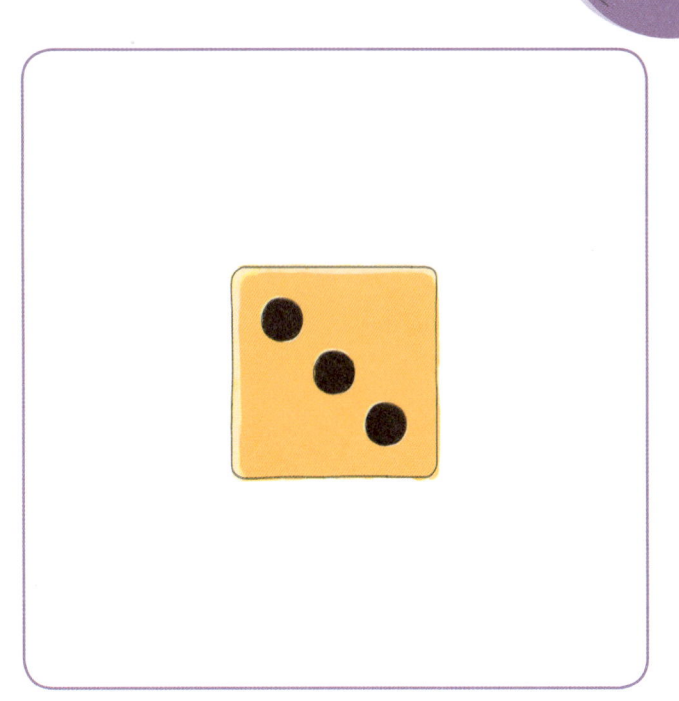

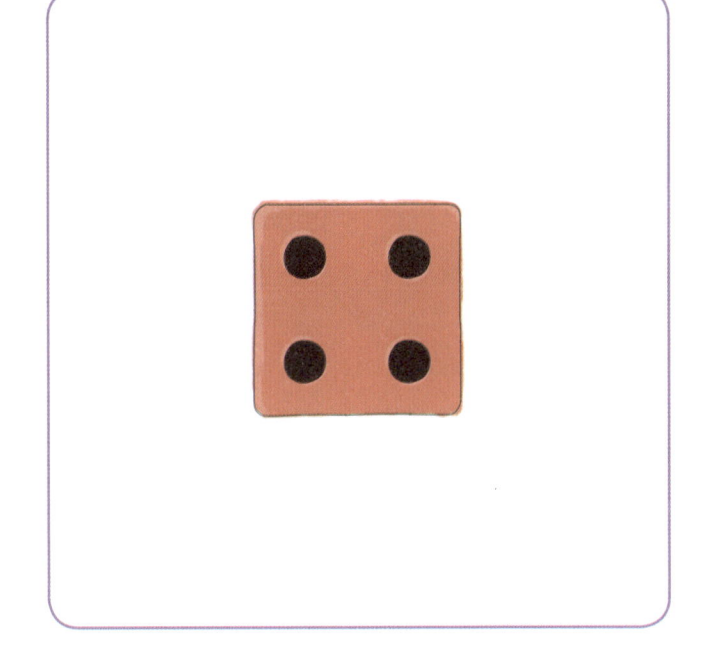

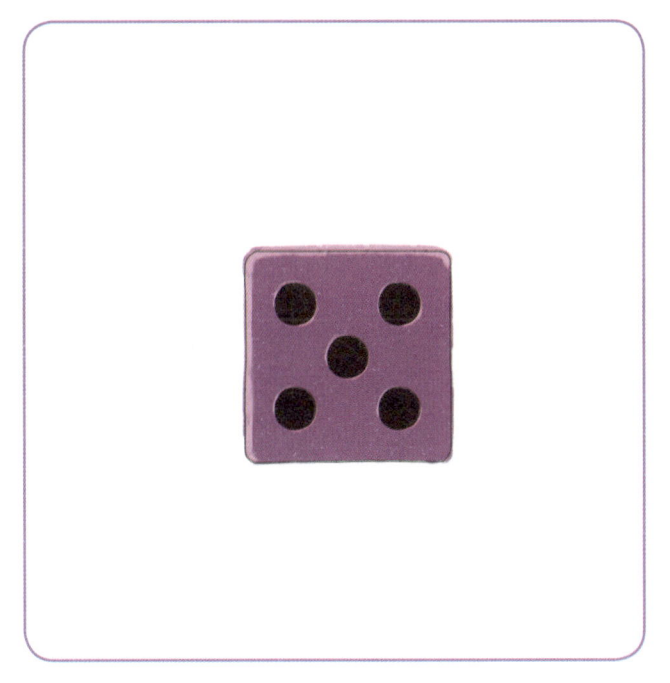

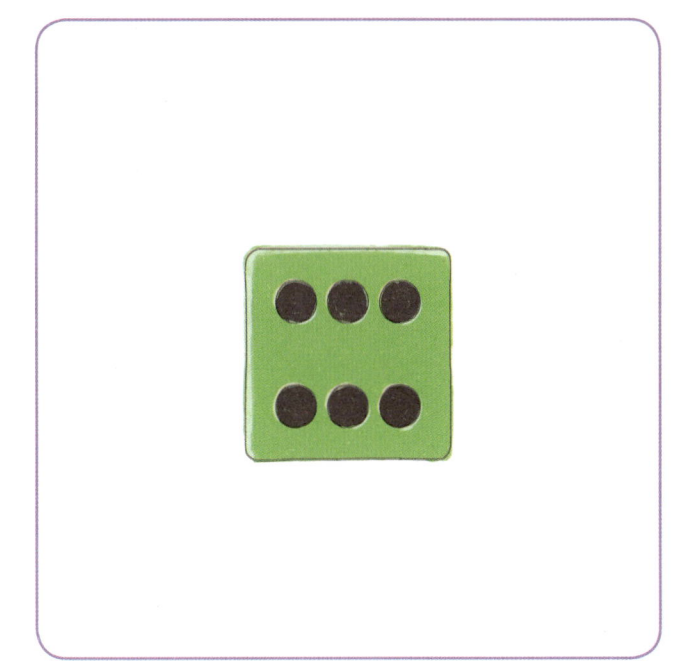

Lesson 2

5 LISTEN AND SING. THEN COUNT AND CIRCLE.

TRACK 17

LESSON 3

6 LOOK, TRACE, AND COLOR.

LESSON 3

7 LISTEN AND CIRCLE.

TRACK 18

Lesson 4

8 MAKE A PIG.

ART & CRAFT CLIL

LESSON 4

UNIT 6 HANSEL AND GRETEL

LESSON 1

1 LOOK AND STICK.

2 LISTEN. THEN FIND AND CIRCLE.

TRACK 19

LESSON 1

3 FINGER-PAINT.

LESSON 2

4 LOOK AND CIRCLE.

LESSON 2

5 LISTEN, SING, AND ACT OUT.

TRACK 20

LESSON 3

SING

6 SAY AND COLOR.

LESSON 3

7. CUT, LISTEN, AND GLUE.

TRACK 21

LESSON 4

1	2	3
4	5	6

8 MAKE A PAPER RAINBOW.

ART & SCIENCE CLIL

LESSON 4

UNIT 7 PINOCCHIO

1 LOOK AND CIRCLE.

2 LISTEN AND STICK.

TRACK 22

LESSON 1

STORY

3 LISTEN AND POINT.

TRACK 23

LESSON 2

4 CUT, GLUE, AND SAY.

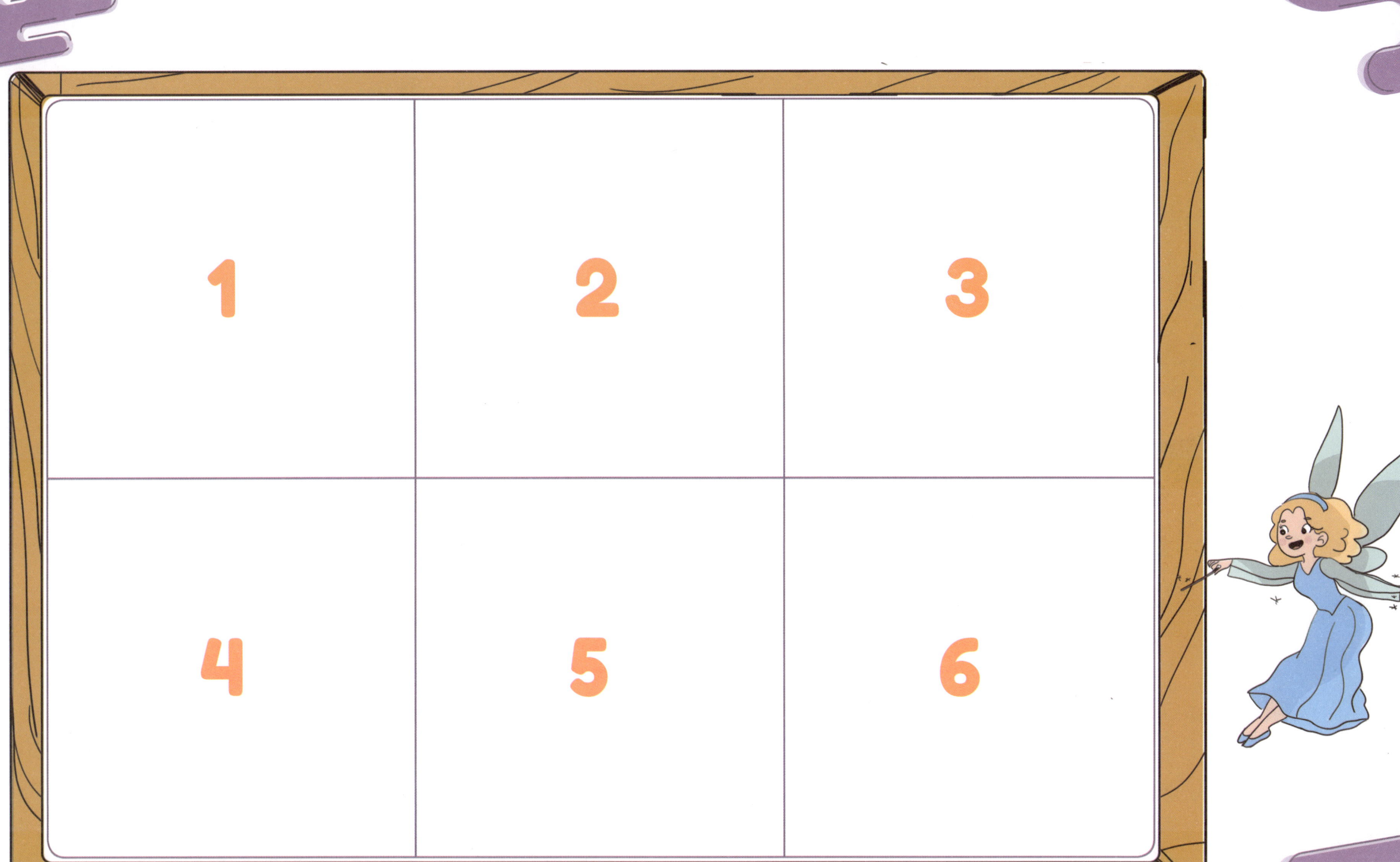

1	2	3
4	5	6

LESSON 2

5 LISTEN, SING, AND ACT OUT.

TRACK 24

LESSON 3

SING

6 TRACE.

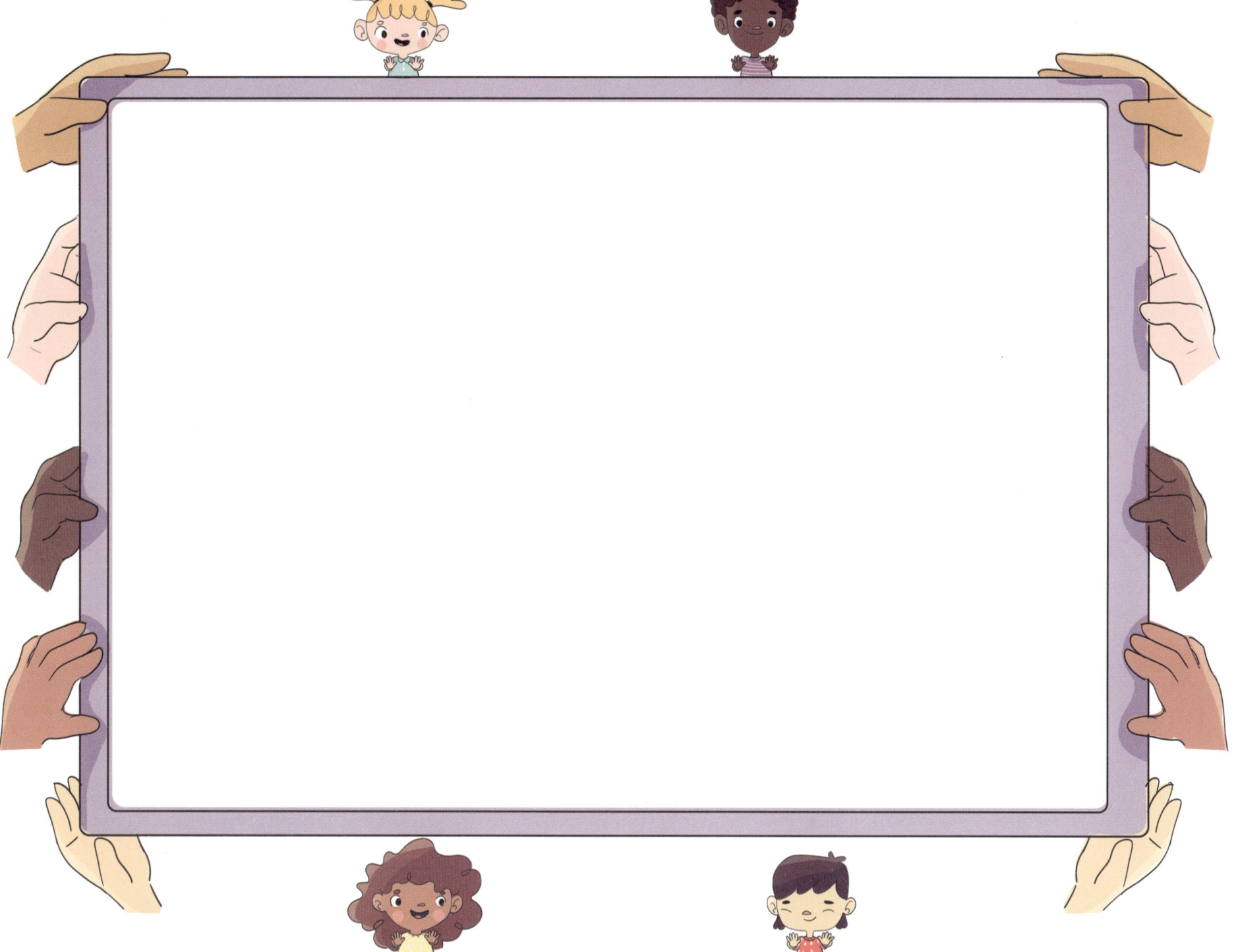

LESSON 3

7 LOOK, POINT, AND SAY.

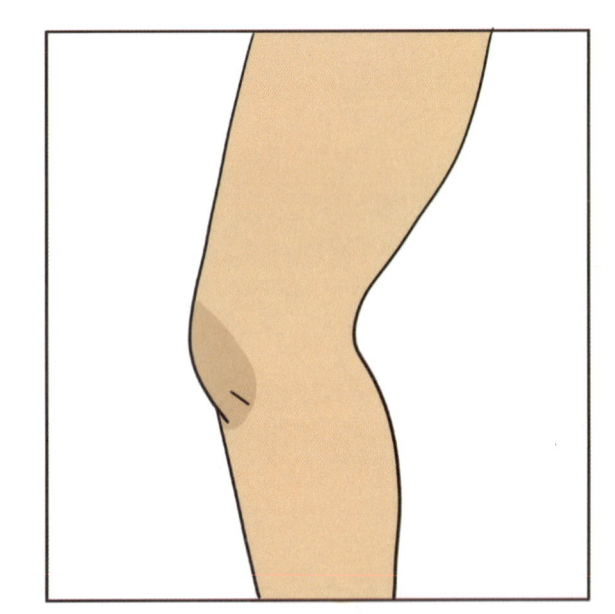

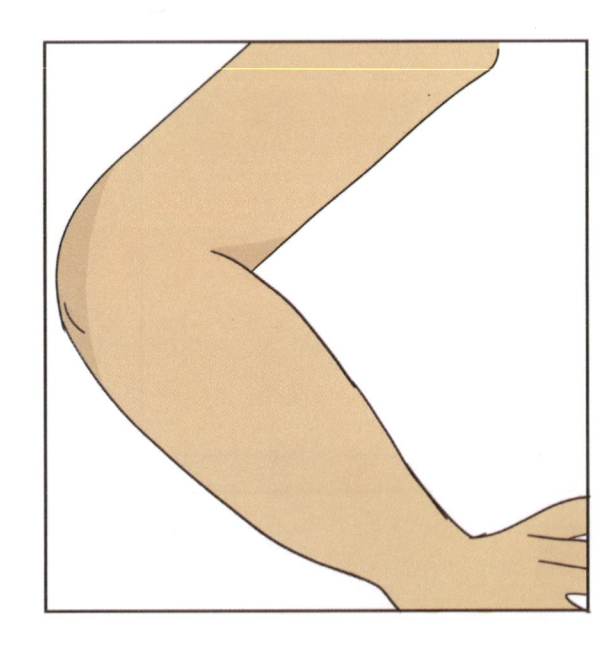

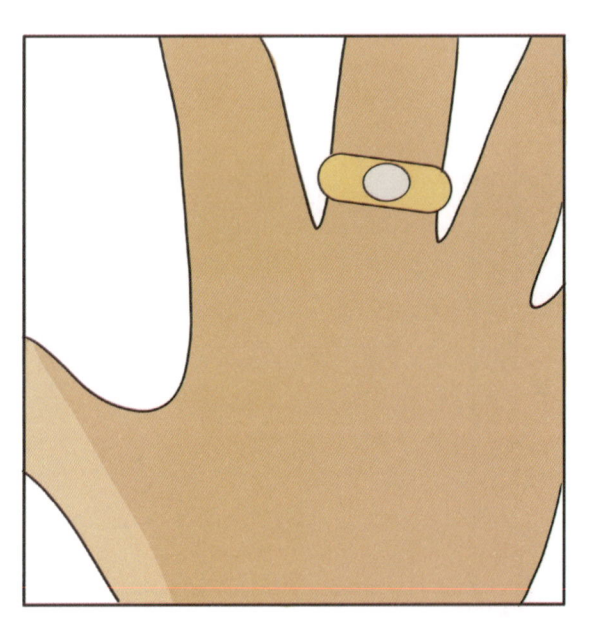

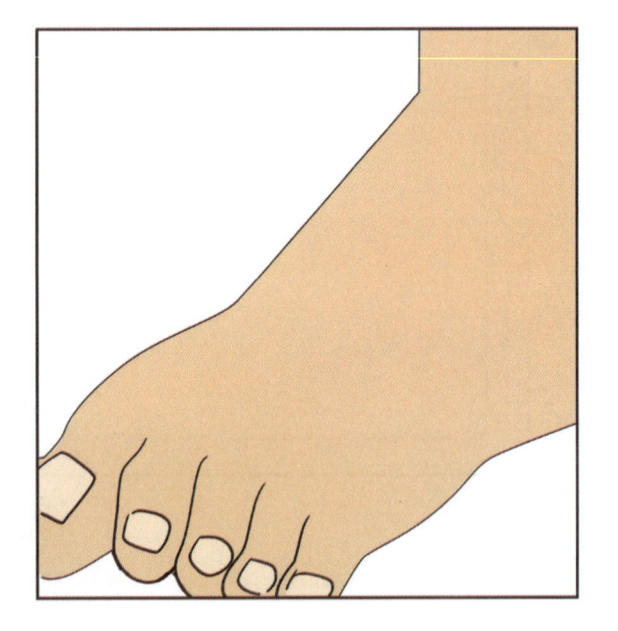

LESSON 4

8 MAKE A PINOCCHIO PUPPET.

ART & SCIENCE CLIL

LESSON 4

Unit 8: The Ant And The Grasshopper

Lesson 1

1 LISTEN AND CIRCLE. TRACK 25

2 LOOK AND STICK.

LESSON 1

STORY

3 LOOK AND MATCH.

LESSON 2

4 COLOR AND SAY.

LESSON 2

5 CUT AND GLUE.

LESSON 3

6 LISTEN, SING, AND ACT OUT.

TRACK 26

LESSON 3

7 LISTEN AND MATCH.

TRACK 27

LESSON 4

8 MAKE HAND PRINT TREES.

ART & CRAFT CLIL

LESSON 4

Press-outs & Stickers

Press-outs

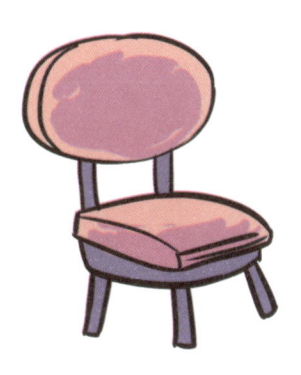

UNIT 1

Press-outs

UNIT 2

Press-Outs

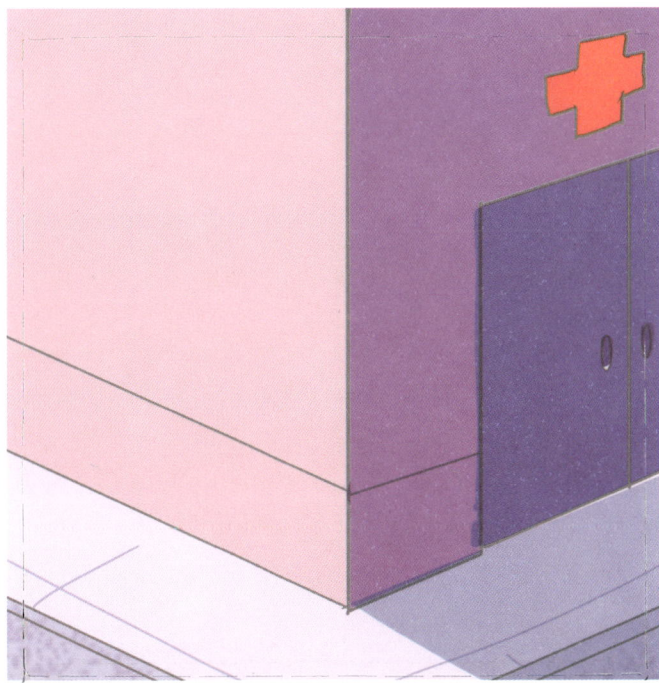

UNIT 3

77

Press-outs

UNIT 4

STORYLAND

Press-outs

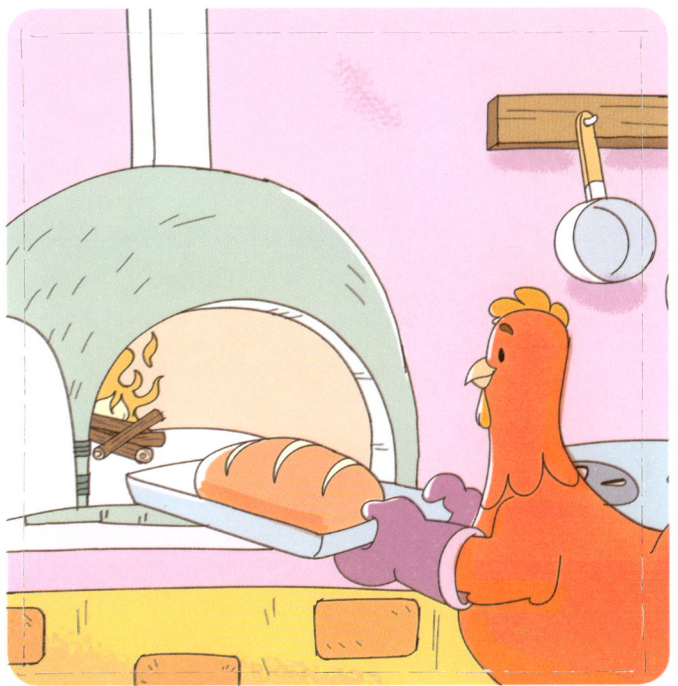

UNIT 5

Press-outs

UNIT 6

Press-outs

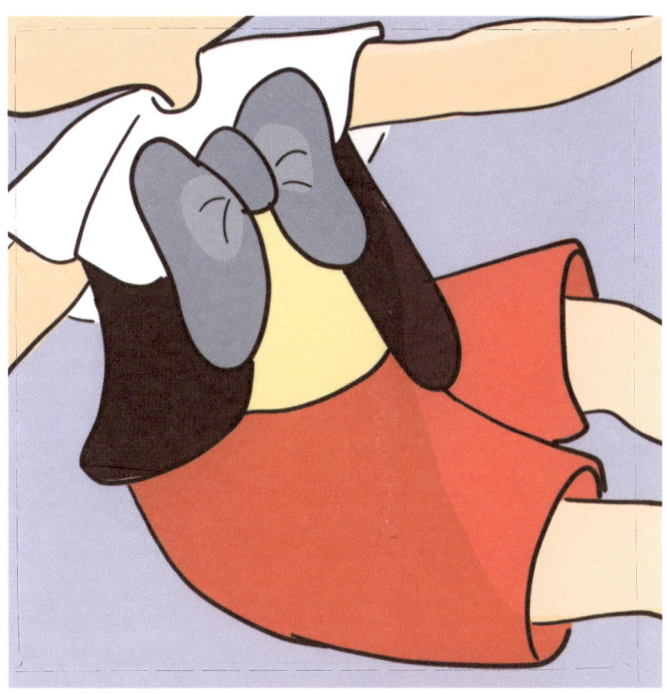

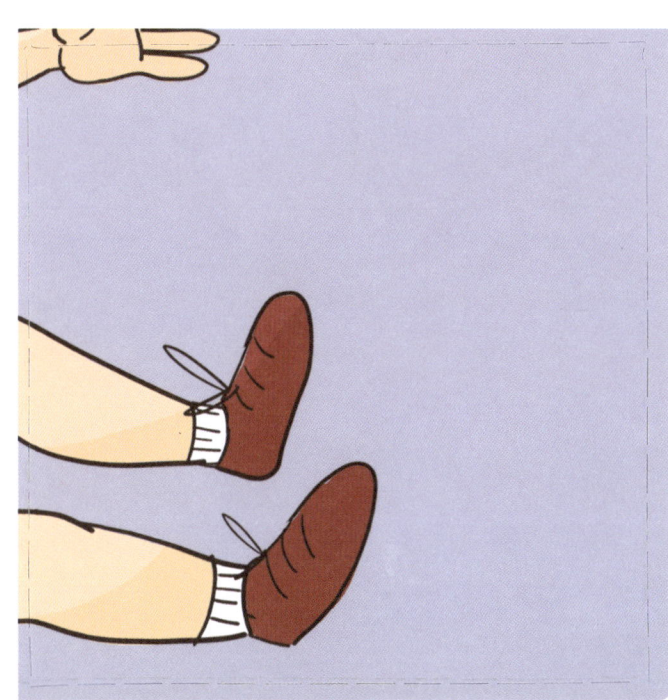

UNIT 7

Press-outs

UNIT 8

ND STORYLAND STORYLAND STORYLAND STORYLAND STORYLAND STORYLAND ST
ORYLAND STORYLAND STORYLAND STORYLAND STORYLAND STORYLAND STORYLA
ND STORYLAND STORYLAND STORYLAND STORYLAND STORYLAND STORYLAND ST
ORYLAND STORYLAND STORYLAND STORYLAND STORYLAND STORYLAND STORYLA
ND STORYLAND STORYLAND STORYLAND STORYLAND STORYLAND STORYLAND ST
ORYLAND STORYLAND STORYLAND STORYLAND STORYLAND STORYLAND STORYLA
ND STORYLAND STORYLAND STORYLAND STORYLAND STORYLAND STORYLAND ST
ORYLAND STORYLAND STORYLAND STORYLAND STORYLAND STORYLAND STORYLA
ND STORYLAND STORYLAND STORYLAND STORYLAND STORYLAND STORYLAND ST
ORYLAND STORYLAND STORYLAND STORYLAND STORYLAND STORYLAND STORYLA
ND STORYLAND STORYLAND STORYLAND STORYLAND STORYLAND STORYLAND ST
ORYLAND STORYLAND STORYLAND STORYLAND STORYLAND STORYLAND STORYLA
ND STORYLAND STORYLAND STORYLAND STORYLAND STORYLAND STORYLAND ST
ORYLAND STORYLAND STORYLAND STORYLAND STORYLAND STORYLAND STORYLA
ND STORYLAND STORYLAND STORYLAND STORYLAND STORYLAND STORYLAND ST
ORYLAND STORYLAND STORYLAND STORYLAND STORYLAND STORYLAND STORYLA
ND STORYLAND STORYLAND STORYLAND STORYLAND STORYLAND STORYLAND ST
ORYLAND STORYLAND STORYLAND STORYLAND STORYLAND STORYLAND STORYLA
ND STORYLAND STORYLAND STORYLAND STORYLAND STORYLAND STORYLAND ST

Stickers

UNIT 1

UNIT 2

Stickers

UNIT 3

UNIT 4

Stickers

UNIT 5

UNIT 6

Stickers

UNIT 7

UNIT 8

Cover Stickers

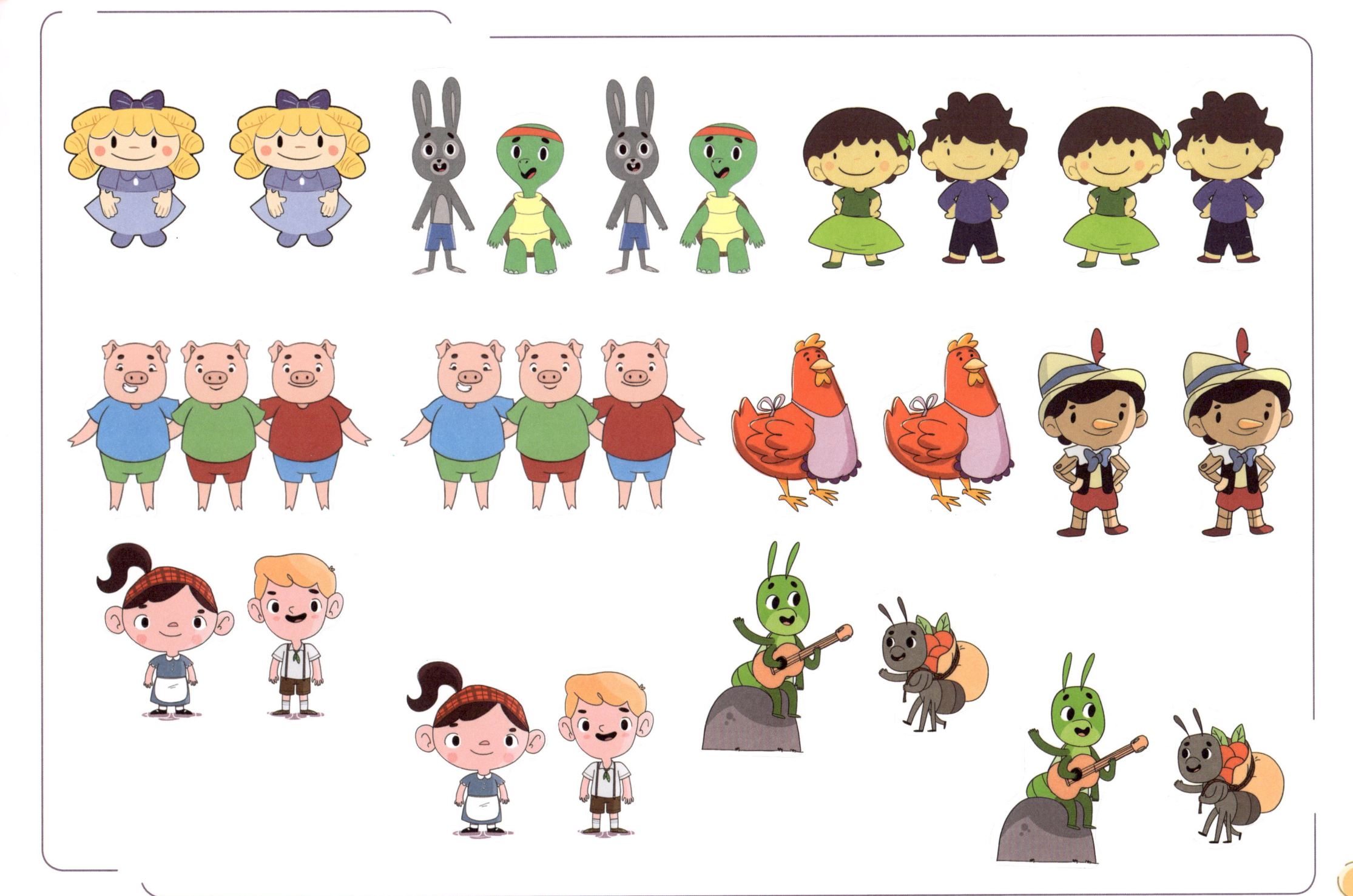